Robert W. James

JavaScript for Absolute Beginners

The introductory programming guide for people who are interested in learning JavaScript but don't have any previous coding experience or programming knowledge

Table of Contents

Introduction..7

Chapter 1: Why JavaScript..11

  What is JavaScript? 11

    High-Level Language..11

    An Interpreted Dynamic Language 13

    Dynamic Variable Typing...14

    Not a Strict Teacher 16

    Client-Side Language...16

    Quick History Lesson..17

Chapter 2: Writing Your First JavaScript Program............19

    How to Write Your First JavaScript Program 19

    Tags..20

    Start Tags and End Tags..22

  More Than Just Displaying Text 25

    Working with Just the Basics 26

    Saving Your Work as HTML...27

Programming Exercises 30

    Inserting the <script> Tag and Pop-Ups 30

    Changing HTML Content...32

    Changing the Style of HTML 33

Pop Quiz 35

  Task..35

    Answer to Pop Quiz...36

Chapter 3: Digging Into the Syntax 37

Case Sensitivity..38

White Space 38

Identifiers...40

Literals..41

Comments 42

Semicolons 43

A Final Word...44

Chapter 4: Modern Markups and External Scripts 45

Type Attribute...45

How to Know If You're Looking at an Old Script........47

External Scripts 48

Creating JavaScript Files..48

Benefits of Using External Scripts 50

Pop Quiz 51

Task...51

Answer to Pop Quiz..52

Chapter 5: Working with Statements 53

What is a Statement in JavaScript? 53

If Else Statement 54

While Statement 54

Do While Statement..55

Continue Statement 56

Break Statement 56

Function Statement 56

Return Statement...57

Var Statement..57

Multiline Comments in JavaScript......................58

Pop Quiz..60

Questions: 60

Chapter 6: Variables and Constants....................61

Const versus Let..61

Declaring Multiple Variables........................63

Pop Quiz...65

Question 65

Answer:..66

Two Lets Produces an Error.............................67

Rules for Naming Variables..............................67

Reserved Words 68

Chapter 7: Data Types and Operators.................70

Dynamically Typed...70

Numbers...70

BigInt...72

Strings..72

Boolean Data Type..73

Null...75

Undefined...75

Object Data Type..76

Symbols 77

Pop Quiz...78

Task...78

Chapter 8: Interacting with Your Users 79

Creating a Prompt...79

Confirm Function...81

Chapter 9: Conditional Statements 83

The If Statement...83

Else Clause 84

Else If Clause 85

The ? Conditional Operator 86

Pop Quiz 89

Task 1 89

Task 2...89

Answer to Pop Quiz Task 1..90

Answer to Pop Quiz Task 2 90

Chapter 10: Looping Statements...91

What is a Loop? 91

The While Loop 91

Single Statement Loops...93

Endless Loop..94

Do...While Loop...94

The For-Loop 95

Inline Variables 97

Global and Local Variables 98

Break and Continue Statements..99

Pop Quiz 102

Task 1 102

Task 2..102

Answer to Pop Quiz Task 1...103

Answer to Pop Quiz Task 2 103

Chapter 11: Functions 105

REMINDER: Local and Global Variables 107

Pop Quiz 108

Task...108

Answer to Pop Quiz..109

Conclusion 110

Introduction

JavaScript is one of the easiest languages to learn for beginners who do not necessarily have any programming background. That is the main assumption of this book—the reader has zero know-how about programming.

It is also assumed that you at least know how to type and compose words on a word processor like MS Word (i.e. Microsoft Word) for instance. It is also assumed that you know how to install applications and also edit whatever you type on the screen—you will be doing that a lot when you work on the exercises and quizzes in this book.

The author of this book also assumes that you already know how to use web browsers and have a good understanding of the World Wide Web. Some readers may have some idea about HTML or Hypertext Markup Language and CSS or Cascading Style Sheets—and that would be a good thing.

But if you don't, well, don't worry about it. We'll go over some essential HTML and other related concepts as we go along. That means you will learn some fundamental HTML programming as well (just the basics, nothing big that will scare non-programmers)

If you're interested in learning how to program in JavaScript, you should also take the time to learn

HTML and CSS because both these programming languages work hand in hand.

JavaScript is a great choice for a beginner programming language. Some people compare it to Python, which is another excellent language for beginners. IMHO, Python is absolutely beginner-friendly and maybe you would want to learn about that too after you've learned a thing or two on JavaScript.

So, why learn JavaScript?

Well, believe it or not, you see it every day. It's there when you look at websites on your laptop's browser. You also experience it when you use your phone. When you interact with the web, you are most likely looking at JavaScript at work. When you use applications that run on the internet, you're already experiencing this programming language first-hand.

If your job happens to involve something about the server-side of any website—maybe you're posting blogs, updating items on your company's online store, or it can be anything that you do on your company's website, then that means you may already be fiddling with a few things JavaScript style.

After you have gained some experience using JavaScript, you will no longer just dip your proverbial toes in the world of web programming. You will learn a thing or two that may be quite amazing. Consider the possibility that you will be doing the following:

- Creating smartwatch applications
- Creating apps for your phone
- Create programs that will be used for micro-controllers
- Create apps that will turn the lights on and off, check out who's knocking at the door, and respond automatically to what users are doing on your website.

Pretty cool, huh?

Remember that this book will teach you the very basic rudiments of JavaScript. Well, we'll throw in a few advanced topics to make things fun and interesting. You will be learning by practice, which means we will include plenty of programming exercises that will help you get the hang of JavaScript.

You will learn things like:

- JavaScript syntax rules
- Variables
- Comments
- Operators
- Math (not fun, I know)
- Functions
- Expressions
- Conditionals
- Values
- And a lot of other fun and neat things

Now, things can get frustrating sometimes, I know. But that's just how things are when you're starting to learn something new. Nevertheless, the journey towards mastering web programming is laced with success and failure—and plenty of JavaScript (big grin!).

Thank you for downloading this book.

I'll see you in chapter 1.

Chapter 1: Why JavaScript

In this chapter, we will learn some background information about one of the most popular programming languages in the world. Let's begin with the characteristics of this programming language.

What is JavaScript?

JavaScript is a high-level language. What does that mean? When we say "high level" we're looking at a programming language that resembles English more than it looks like a bunch of code that only a machine can understand. It doesn't look like the scrolling characters that you see on the screen when you watch any of the Matrix trilogy movies.

High-Level Language

When you look at the lines of code you will see English words mixed with a bunch of math on them. The JavaScript computer code will also look like a coded message with hidden meanings. However, after some practice, you will notice that the coded message part of the language is pretty easy to figure out.

Now, let's go in a bit deeper.

When you say high-level language, we're looking at a programming language where you don't need to bother with the other technical details going on behind the scenes. For example, when you tell the computer to display the letter "A" on the browser or the screen, you don't see exactly how the program is telling the computer or mobile device (like your phone for instance) just how to do that.

Here are a few things that you don't get to see happening. First off, one of the things that go on in the background is that your program (any program, it doesn't have to be JavaScript) is telling the computer to use a certain part of its random access memory.

It will also tell the computer to activate certain pixels on the screen. It also tells the computer which part of the screen will be used to display the letter A. Your program also tells the computer what color to use. It also tells the computer which pixels should be used to create that specific display.

All of that is already handled in the background. All you ever did is type one command or line of code that says "display the letter A" on the screen.

A high-level computer language allows you to focus on the code. It does the rest of the dirty work for you.

An Interpreted Dynamic Language

Remember that JavaScript resembles English more than Matrix-like code (i.e. machine code) – yes, continuing the pun right there. The thing about that is the fact that machines don't understand English. They don't talk that way—they use binary code, a series of ones, and zeroes (or on and off switches).

No, you don't need to learn binary code to program in JavaScript. But just remember this important tidbit—you need to translate your computer program from a high-level language to a low-level language or machine code.

There is usually a go-between or a translator if you will between high-level programming languages and machine-readable language. This "translation" in programming is called compilation.

The code that you wrote in any programming language needs to be compiled (i.e. translated) so that the computer (or phone or any device) can follow the instructions that you have written.

In certain programming languages, you need to go through this step first before your computer can execute the instructions. These languages are called static languages. There should be a compile-time first before the execution.

That is not the case with JavaScript.

It's called an "interpreted language" because there is no need for a translation process in between.

The code you write in this programming language is "translated" on the fly, as it were, or as the code is read. It's that fast. There is no need to pause anything first so the code can be compiled. That is why it is called a dynamic language.

Now, this offers a few advantages, such as:

- Closures
- Object runtime alternation
- Functional programming
- Reflection
- Late binding
- Dynamic typing

Don't worry about all those terms for now. You will learn them later as we go along with the lessons in JavaScript programming. We'll work on the related jargon as we go through the different chapters.

Dynamic Variable Typing

Do you remember variables in math? I'm referring to algebra to be specific. As a quick review: a variable is something that holds or contains a value. Like sometimes we assign x = 10 for example. The variable x contains an integer value. An integer is a number that doesn't contain a fractional part—like 0.5 or 0.75 for example.

So, in this example, x only contains the value of 10 – no decimal points whatsoever. Once you assign something else to the variable x then it changes. So, let's say we add a 0.5 to x then it becomes a real number since its value is 10.5.

In certain programming languages, like Pascal, Basic, C, or C++ for instance, if you assign a variable a specific type (like an integer for instance, which follows our previous explanation) that variable can only contain whole numbers or integers.

If you try to change that along the way then it will produce an error and the program fails. That means if you assign the value of 10 to the variable "x" then this variable can't contain any fractional or decimal parts.

You will have to create a different variable for the real number, which is the case for many static programming languages.

But that is not the case with JavaScript. You can assign 10 at the beginning of your code and then add the 0.3 later on and it will not create any problems. This is called dynamic typing. It is a convenient way to work with variables and also to reduce run time errors when a computer, phone, or some other device runs your program.

Not a Strict Teacher

As you can see so far, JavaScript is not as we say a strict programming language. The usual restrictive rules that are present in other languages have been done away with here. This allows learners beginners in programming to make the usual "mistakes" in programming.

You get to focus on the foundational concepts of programming without having to worry about a lot of rules about program structure where this part of the code goes where or which thing goes where.

It is very beginner-friendly, which is why JavaScript is a great choice for beginners who want to learn web programming.

NOTE: take note that JavaScript is a different programming language compared to Java. They sound the same and the naming convention is a truly bad practice but we can't do anything about it. Everyone just has to live with that. Just remember that we're learning JavaScript and not the other full-blown computer programming language called Java.

Client-Side Language

This scripting language is also referred to as a client-side language. This means that a lot of its features are to be used for the benefit of the computer user. In contrast with that, a server-side language is more concerned about what happens in the background of a website—particularly on the servers where these sites are contained. There are other client-side and server-side languages out there as well.

In the case of JavaScript, this programming language is often used for improving the interaction between a website and the users that visit them. The program code that you will make from this language will make things more interactive.

That is why it is used in other places as well other than just websites. It is used in mobile application development and games as well. The apps and games on your phone and other mobile devices need to be interactive and JavaScript is a powerful way to help you do that.

Quick History Lesson

Let's get over this part quickly so we can move on to the actual code writing. Here's a quick overview of the history of this programming language:

- It was developed in 1995 by Brendan Eich
- It was originally called LiveScript but was later changed to JavaScript

- A lot of the syntax of JavaScript was taken from or influenced by the C programming language
- Today it has been developed to run not just on computers but you will find many embedded applications, web browser applications, TV apps, and of course mobile apps.

If you want to delve deeper into the history of this programming language, then you should look for it other sources. There is plenty of history and language development information elsewhere.

Now, let's get into the nitty-gritty stuff, shall we?

See you in chapter 2

Chapter 2: Writing Your First JavaScript Program

In this chapter, we will go over and write your first JavaScript program—or programs, since you will be working on several exercises at the end of this chapter. Here you will learn a few basic but really important concepts. In this chapter, we will go over what you need to write and run your JavaScript programs and the first few elements of the JavaScript syntax.

How to Write Your First JavaScript Program

I always say that the best way to learn something new is to simply just jump into it get things done. And that is what we're going to do right now—make you write your first JavaScript program and see what happens.

So, what do you need to run a JavaScript program?

You will need two things to run JavaScript, which are the following:

1. A text editor such as Atom, Sublime Text, Visual Studio Code, and Notepad++.
2. A browser like Chrome, Safari, Firefox, and Microsoft Edge

Any of these text editors will work nicely. I don't recommend simple text editors since all you can do with those things is type up words. The editors mentioned above double up as source code editors' features, which means they autocorrect (and autocomplete) your programming code syntax.

I'll be displaying code using Notepad++ in this book, which is a text and source code editor that is free and easy to download.

You can download Notepad++ by clicking here.

Downloading and installing it on your computer takes less than a minute.

Remember that JavaScript is a scripting language, which means it can't run programs on its own. In this setup, you type the program code in the text editor and it is your browser's job to interpret and run the code.

JavaScript is also a very portable language since it runs in any operating system including Windows, iOS, Android, Mac, and Linux among others.

Tags

Now, here's a new concept that some readers will learn for the first time. Parts of your code will be enclosed in an opening and closing tag. Here's an example:

<script> and </script>

The first one is <script> which shows you where the code begins or where the tag begins and the second one, which is </script>, shows you where the tag ends. You use those two tags to tell the browser that whatever is in between those two tags is a form of a script—in the case of our little activity here we're using JavaScript.

Yes, there are other scripting languages as well such as Ruby, Python, Perl, and PHP among others. If you have played around with bb-codes used in forums, it's pretty much the same concept.

For instance, you use the [b] and [/b] tag so that the text inside the script is displayed in bold typeface. So, for example, when you write the following in an online forum post:

"Hi! My name is [b]Jeff [/b]."

It will be displayed in the forums as "Hi! My name is **Jeff**." As you can see, the word Jeff is in bold characters.

Now, I hope that you have downloaded Notepad++ or some other source code editor. If you haven't, then it's time to download one now and install it on your computer. After installing one (remember I'm using Notepad++ coz it's free), type the following in that code editor:

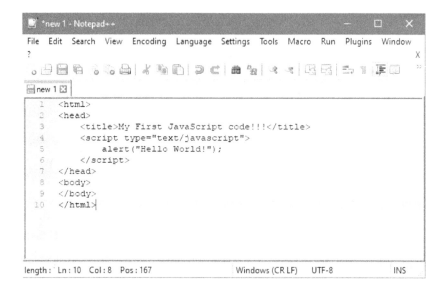

Here are a few things that you should notice about the sample code above. First off, the first line says <html> which means that this is an HTML program; HTML stands for HyperText Markup Language, which is the main language used for building web pages. As it was mentioned earlier, you will learn a few things about that programming language.

Start Tags and End Tags

If you go over our example earlier, you will see that the entire code begins with <html> and is paired at the bottom by another tag which is </html>. The former is called the start tag and the latter is called the end tag.

The same is true with JavaScript. Your JavaScript code also has a start tag and an end tag. Other start and end tag pairs in our example above are <title> and </title>, <head> and </head>, <script> and </script>, and <body> and </body>.

Note that the majority of the tags in our first example are HTML. The JavaScript actually begins with <script type="text/javascript"> and ends with </script.

Now, take note that this script format works for HTML, not HTML5, which is different.

Here's another example, and I want you to identify the different start and end tags:

```
1    <html>
2
3        <head>
4            <title>Nested Elements Example</title>
5        </head>
6
7        <body>
8            <h1>This is <i>italic</i> heading</h1>
9            <p>This is <u>underlined</u> paragraph</p>
10       </body>
11
12   </html>
```

After identifying the different tags, here are a few things that you need to note:

- The code begins with the <html> tag and ends with the </html> tag.
- The <head> and </head> tags indicate the metadata. This is called the <head> element and it is not displayed on your browser or device screen. This serves as the title of your HTML document—or title of your program as it were.
- The <h1> and </h1> tags are the headers. Think of these as paragraph titles or headings of chapters in a book.
- The <p> and </p> tags indicate the paragraph elements. They tell the browser where a paragraph begins and ends.
- The <i> and </i> tags display text in italics and the <u> and </u> tags display text in underlined texts.
- The <body> and </body> tags identify the body element or the body of the document— earlier we have a head element and now we have a body element. Observe that the body element should always be in between the <html> and <body> tags.

We will learn more about the interplay of HTML and JavaScript as we go along with the chapters of this book. If you run the code in our second example, it would display something like this on your browser.

This is *italic* heading

This is <u>underlined</u> paragraph

More Than Just Displaying Text

JavaScript does more than just display text on your screen. It is that part of your website that makes it more interactive. Create a new file on Notepad++ and type the following:

```
*new 3 - Notepad++
File  Edit  Search  View  Encoding  Language  Settings  Tools  Macro  Run  Plugins  Window  ?

new 3

 1   <!DOCTYPE html>
 2   <html>
 3   <body>
 4
 5   <h2>Welcome to JavaScript!</h2>
 6
 7   <button type="button"
 8   onclick="document.getElementById('demo').innerHTML = Date()">
 9   Click me to display Date and Time.</button>
10
11   <p id="demo"></p>
12
13   </body>
14   </html> |

length : 241   lines : 14        Ln : 14   Col : 9   Pos : 242        Windows (CR LF)   UTF-8        INS
```

Working with Just the Basics

If you don't want to bother with all the HTML code mentioned earlier and just want to learn the fundamentals of JavaScript just remember that all you need is this basic skeleton tag format:

```
File  Edit  Search  View  Encoding  Language  Settings  Tools  Macro  Run  Plugins  Window  ?                        X
new 1
1    <html>
2
3    <script>
4
5    ...
6
7    </script>
8
9    </html>

length : 49   lines : 9        Ln : 9   Col : 8   Pos : 50              Windows (CR LF)   UTF-8              INS
```

Those are the only four tags that you need and all you have to do is to insert your JavaScript code (or scripts for short) in between the script tags (i.e. where the ellipses are).

But if you want to add some text elements you are free to use content within <p>and <h1>, and <h2> tags. Your scripts will still work even if you have those text elements.

Saving Your Work as HTML

The next thing you need to do is to click File > Save As and then in the window that comes up click Desktop in the panel on the left so you save your work on the desktop. You can choose a different folder if you like.

After that, click on Save as Type and select HyperText Markup Language File from the drop-down, and under file name write Welcome to JavaScript. You will see a new file on your desktop (or your selected folder) called "Welcome to JavaScript" and it will have the icon of your default browser—mine is Google Chrome so I see a new Chrome file on my desktop.

Double click on that file and your default browser will open it. On your browser you will see the following displayed:

Welcome to JavaScript!

Click me to display Date and Time.

Notice that there is a button there as well. The welcome message is in bold typeface and is in the style of a header, which is because of the <h2> tags. Now, click on the button. You will see that the current date and time in your place will be displayed on the screen.

As you can see, JavaScript makes the page more interactive rather than just display text on the screen.

As a recap, we learned the following:

- JavaScript is embedded in HTML documents and that these two programming languages almost resemble one another.
- Tags always come in pairs
- Some tags are positioned in between other tags.

- JavaScript code begins and ends with the <script> tags.
- JavaScript makes web pages more interactive

Programming Exercises

In this section, before we jump into chapter 2 of this book, you will learn a bit more of the interactive features that can be added to the web pages that you will build. Remember that we will only focus on the core of JavaScript and we will only mention HTML and also CSS in passing.

We will keep the browser-specific commands to a bare minimum. This means we will not deal with features of this language such as documents, events, and interfaces. We may mention them in passing and provide some examples but we're not going to focus on them.

Remember that this book is about JavaScript basics for beginners. We focus only on the fundamental groundwork that you will need as someone new to programming in general.

Going back to the subject of this subsection, we will go over a few more program examples that will show you the interactive features of this programming language.

Inserting the <script> Tag and Pop-Ups

Remember that you can insert your JavaScript code almost anywhere in an HTML code using the <script>

tag. Enter the following code in Notepad++ and save it as HTML.

```
<!DOCTYPE HTML>
<html>

<body>

  <p>This is HTML before the script...</p>

  <script>
    alert( 'This is a pop-up!' );
  </script>

  <p>And this is HTML after the script.</p>

</body>

</html>
```

You can name it any way you want. Open the HTML file using your browser. Notice that when you open it, you will see a pop-up with the message "This is a pop-up". Click the OK button and then you will see some text displayed on your browser window.

If you inspect the code that you wrote, the JavaScript code was inserted in between two HTML programming lines—the ones that say before the script and after the script (lines 6 and 12).

This is just a demonstration of how you can insert JavaScript in between HTML. Notice, line 9 in our sample code has "alert" in it, which is a browser-specific command. We use that command to display text. Pay attention to its syntax. You can use single quotes or double quotes for the text that will be displayed.

We will go over the rules on syntax in chapter 3 of this book.

Changing HTML Content

Here's another interactive thing that you can do with JavaScript: change the content on a webpage. Create a new file on Notepad++ and enter the following code. Pay attention to the syntax for the button element. We will go over the elements of that element later. For now, we will focus on this feature of JavaScript.

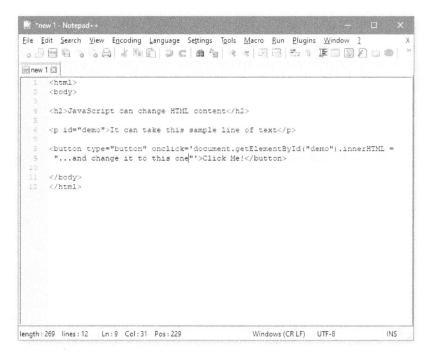

Save your work as an HTML file and use whatever name you want to. Open that file by double-clicking it and it will open up your default browser.

Note that you will see the header at the top (i.e. the text in the <h2> tag). Underneath that is a line of text followed by a "click me" button. When you click the button, notice that the text is changed to the one specified on the button click.

Changing the Style of HTML

The HTML code that you write has certain styles. These styles show how the content of the web page will be presented to the site visitor. JavaScript can change the styles on how a page is presented.

Here's an example that you can try. Copy the following in a new document in Notepad++, save it as an HTML file, and open the document in your browser.

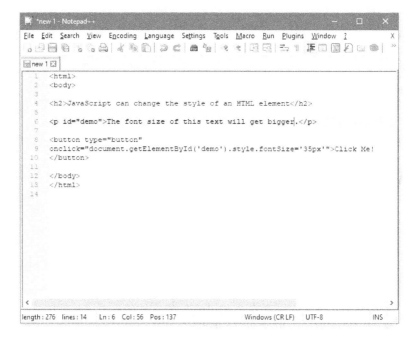

Watch when you click the button. The font size of the text changes after you click it.

Pop Quiz

This is our first pop quiz. You will get a few more of these as we go along with the lessons in this book. The question will be provided here and you will find the answer on the next page.

Task

Create a web page document that will display the message "I'm JavaScript!" Use the information provided so far and also the tidbits from the examples that we have provided.

Save your work as an HTML file and open your file in your browser.

Answer to Pop Quiz

```
<html>

<body>

  <script>
    alert( "I'm JavaScript!" );
  </script>

</body>

</html>
```

Chapter 3: Digging Into the Syntax

We have gone through some of the basics about the syntax of JavaScript in the previous chapter. We will concentrate on that a little bit more in this chapter. Note that compared to a lot of other programming languages out there, the syntax used in this one is rather simple.

When we say syntax, we are referring to the rules on how words and symbols are supposed to be arranged in JavaScript. If you form or arrange these linguistic elements correctly then the program code that you wrote will be interpreted correctly by the browser and it will perform exactly as you have instructed.

However, if you made a mistake in the syntax, it will produce an error. The good news is that there are only a few syntactical rules that we need to cover. There are only five headings on syntax that you need to learn as a beginner, which includes the following:

- Case sensitivity
- White space
- Identifiers
- Literals
- Comments
- Semicolons

Let's start with the easiest subject, case sensitivity.

Case Sensitivity

JavaScript is a case-sensitive language. This means that when you use words, the way you capitalize letters will count. For instance, let's say you want to save the passwords that website users enter into something called a variable (more on that later) and you call this password "Password".

That is how it should appear throughout your program. If you used "password" for any reason in your program code, it will be seen as something different from "Password". Remember that "password" will be treated as something different from "Password". The upper case and lower case letters will differentiate things in your code.

White Space

White space refers to the spaces, line breaks, and tab stops that you make when you type something in any document. We usually just use one space after each word that we type. If we put in two spaces when we type things in MS Word, for instance, then the spell checker will prompt you that you have made that typographical error.

Well, in JavaScript, those spaces and tabs don't matter. That is why you can type as many spaces as you like and it won't cause any errors. In theory, you can add as many of these elements as you like and it won't be a problem.

In practice, there is an unwritten law or practice if you will amongst programmers as to how you will format every code that you will write. What we're looking for is an organized looking code to make it more readable. You don't want your code to look like all the parts are headed in every direction possible.

Consider our first sample code earlier, which you will see here:

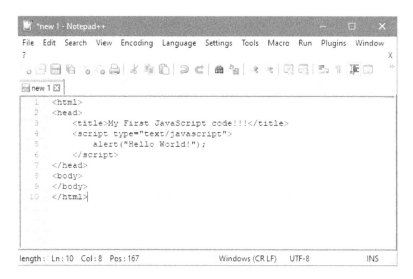

As you can see from this example, everything is aligned to the left. If an element is nested within another element you indent it. For example, look at the sample code above. You will see that after the <head> element, everything is indented 1 tab space.

Lines 3 to 6 in the code above are indented. That means they are found within the <head> element. Everything goes back to the left alignment in line 7 where the </head> tag is located.

Now, look at line 5 of the code above. You will see that the line

alert("Hello World!");

It is nested inside the <script> tags. You've seen this statement before in chapter 2. Here's what you need to remember—in practice, you are supposed to indent or nest everything that belongs inside another element. Doing that makes finding specific code elements a lot easier.

This practice also makes it easier for you to spot bugs in your program. By bugs, we refer to errors in our code. Don't worry; it happens to the best of us. We all make mistakes when we write our code.

Identifiers

An identifier is a word or character that you, the programmer, will supply. These are characters and words that you will use to identify different elements of a program. In essence, they are the names that you give to different parts of a program.

Going back to an earlier example, let's say that you want website visitors to enter a password when they use your site (just like what Facebook or other web portals do). Let's say that we want to store the password in a variable which we will call simply as Password. That is one example of an identifier and this one is called a variable, which is a program element that stores certain values—yes, just like in algebra.

An identifier in JavaScript can be a string of letters. You can also use only one character like x or y—yes, just like math again. Your identifiers can start with any letter and it can also start with an underscore.

So let's say we use _Password to store the passwords supplied by users, then that identifier is perfectly legal in the syntactical rules of JavaScript.

Some identifiers start with a $ sign. However, do take note that we use the $ sign in JavaScript to reference DOM elements. We'll cover DOM elements in a later chapter of this book.

Literals

The next syntax rules that we will go over are for literals in JavaScript. Earlier we mentioned that there are variables in JavaScript. Our previous example is the variable which we called Password. This variable is the one that we will use to store the passwords supplied by website visitors.

Literals are the actual values that will be assigned to variables. Let's say we have assigned the variable Password to contain "12345678" as the default password. The value "12345678" is called a literal.

It is the value that we assign to these variables and other program elements. Literals don't need to be numbered. It can be letters or a combination of letters and numbers. More advanced literal constructs that we will cover later on include array literals, Boolean literals, and others.

For now, don't think about the advanced stuff just yet. We'll get to that soon enough. For now, just think of literals as the values that you will assign to different programming elements using your source code.

Remember that we will only deal with the basics for now in this book. No headache making advanced topics just yet.

Comments

Check out the following code and try to look for the comments in it.

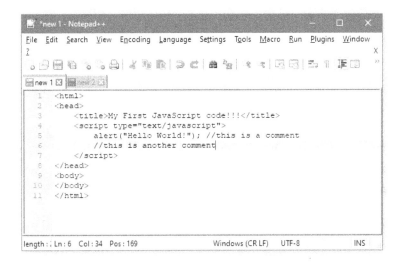

As you can see in the sample code above, there is a comment on line 5 and another one in line 6. Note that these comments will not be treated as programming code. A comment is a description or a note that is intended for the program author or the one editing or updating the code.

Think of them as annotations that will make it easier for you to understand the structure of your code and to help you know what each part of the code does. This will be helpful in the future in case you need to update your code or make certain changes to make it better.

Semicolons

Go back to line 5 of our sample code, the one before the comment. The code goes like this:

```
alert("Hello World!");
```

If you guessed that this line tells the browser to display "Hello World!" on the screen, then you're right. That is what "alert" does—we'll cover that later. What I want you to notice is that this line ended with a semicolon.

Remember that every line of program code that you write in JavaScript should end with a semicolon. The rest of the program code in our example above is HTML and it doesn't require a semicolon at the end. But if you're writing the JavaScript part, then you must end the commands with a semicolon or it will cause an error.

A Final Word

And that is pretty much it when it comes to the syntax rules in JavaScript. If you need to review them then you can read this entire chapter all over again. Note that many of the syntax rules that we have covered here are also the same rules in other programming languages.

Chapter 4: Modern Markups and External Scripts

We went over the details of the syntax used in JavaScript and also that for HTML as well. As a bit of a footnote to that discussion, you should know that there are old scripting rules and there are modern ones in use today.

Why do we still stick with the old stuff? Well, this is because of old websites that still haven't been updated yet—or maybe never. The <script> tag, which we still use today, has some of those old attributes which are no longer applicable.

Type Attribute

In one of the examples that we used (the very first one actually), we used a "type" attribute. Here's the sample code that used that attribute:

It is in line 4. You insert this line in the <script> tag:

type="text/javascript"

Note that this attribute is no longer required in modern markup languages like JavaScript. This is because our browsers have been updated and have since made those features obsolete.

That attribute no longer makes sense, because what it does is that tells your browser that the type of script being used in your HTML code is JavaScript. That used to make sense when there were other competing scripts. But nowadays, JavaScript is the default scripting language, so using that attribute doesn't do a thing since your browsers already use JavaScript by default.

If you check the other examples in the exercises that we worked on, notice that they do not contain "type" anymore and the code still works.

How to Know If You're Looking at an Old Script

If you pursue a career in web development you may be tasked with editing old code. Sometimes your tasks will involve updating websites that have a combination of old and new code—it happens.

There are ways to determine if you're working on old code. In the case of JavaScript, one of the easy ways that you can find out is when you see comments before and after the script. We talked about comments in chapter 3, remember?

Programmers used to add comments before and after their scripts. Here's an example of that:

```
<script type="text/javascript"><!--
    ...
//--></script>
```

What are comments used for again? Remember that browsers do not treat comments as programming code so they are not executed or performed like regular instructions. Back in the day, programmers used comments to hide the scripts so that older browsers won't have any trouble interpreting the code for their web pages.

Well, nowadays we no longer have that problem so you don't need to "hide" your JavaScript using comments. That means if ever you are tasked to edit old website code, you can just remove those comments to see what the script is supposed to do.

External Scripts

Let's say you have lots of scripts and you usually use the same scripts from one web page to the next. It will be quite repetitive to write all that code over and over again, right? The good news is that there is a way to save the JavaScript code that you use regularly and you just reference them in your new code or page so you don't have to retype or copy-paste everything over and over.

What you need to do is to save your scripts in external files.

Creating JavaScript Files

To create your JavaScript files, you just type your script codes, as usual, the same way you've been doing it like in the exercises we've worked on. After typing up your scripts instead of saving them as an HTML file as we used to do it, we save them as a JavaScript file. It will have a ".js" extension instead.

You can save them in the same local directory as the HTML files that you create or you can reference them using the directory path or folder where they are saved. If you save them in your site's server, then you should use the URL of the directory on your server.

To reference the JavaScript files that you create, use the src attribute. Here's an example of an src statement:

```
<script src="/path/to/script.js"></script>
```

In this example, the part that goes /path/to/ is the directory path or folder where your script file is located and script.js is the name that was given to the JavaScript file that you saved. Of course, you can use a different directory path and file name.

Now, let's say that your script file and your HTML code are saved in the same directory. You don't need to write the entire directory path. So, in the case of our example, you don't need to include "/path/to/" in the src attribute. You can write your reference as

```
<script src="script.js"></script>
```

This means that the script file you created is saved in the current active directory. Now, here's an example of src attribute referencing an actual file in a server:

```
<script
src="https://cdnjs.cloudflare.com/ajax/libs/lodash.js/4.17.11/lodash.js"></script>
```

If you want to use several script files in your code, then just reference each one of them using separate src statements. Here's an example:

```
<script src="/myfiles/script1.js"></script>
<script src="/myfiles/script2.js"></script>
```

In the example above, the script files are saved in the "myfiles" folder. The names of the scripts are script1.js and script2.js.

Benefits of Using External Scripts

The rule of thumb here is that you should only write the short and simple JavaScripts on the actual code for each web page. The longer and more complex scripts should be saved in separate JavaScript files.

You will reference them in your code only when you need them. This helps to keep your web page code shorter. There is another benefit to using external scripts—it makes web pages load a lot faster.

How does it do that? Whenever someone opens your web page or website, that user's browser will automatically download the scripts and save them in the browser cache. That means the scripts are already loaded in their browser every time they visit your site.

They no longer need to download the entire file for your site thus making page loads a lot faster. If the same script is going to be used on another web page, then the browser doesn't need to download it again since it is already saved in the cache.

Pop Quiz

Task

Create a script file that will use the alert statement and display the text "I'm JavaScript!"

Remember to save it as a JavaScript file instead of an HTML file. **HINT:** you can use the same file you created from our first pop quiz earlier. After saving it, create another script but this time save it as an HTML file. Reference the script file that you created in the previous step.

Open the new file using your browser.

You will find the answer on the next page.

Answer to Pop Quiz

This is the answer for the JavaScript file, which is saved with the file name alert.js:

This file is saved in the same active directory as the HTML file that we will create later on that will reference this script.

Here is the answer for the script that references the file above:

Chapter 5: Working with Statements

You have been introduced to and have used two statements so far, namely the alert and src statements. In this chapter, we will cover the statements used in JavaScript and how they will affect your web pages.

What is a Statement in JavaScript?

To answer this question, try to go back to how the alert and src statements behave in the scripts that you have written so far. The alert statement displays text while the src statement will reference or make use of code saved in external JavaScript files.

What is common about these two? If you answered that they perform actions then you are correct. A statement in JavaScript is a line of code that makes a browser to perform certain actions.

In short, statements are commands.

You can tell that a line of code is a statement by the semicolon at the end. The semicolons separate one statement from another. Statements are translated by a browser one line at a time.

The following are some of the most common JavaScript statements that you ought to know as a beginner. We will go over these statements again as we discuss the different programming elements later on.

If Else Statement

This is a conditional statement. It will test a certain logical condition if it is true or not. For example, if a user wants to log into their account on your website, they will need to enter the correct password for that account.

After entering their password, your script can test if what they entered matches the password that is stored on your website. If it is a match then they are allowed access or else they will be prompted to try again and enter the right password.

While Statement

This is a type of looping statement. A loop is a programming construct that repeats a statement or a block of statements over and over as long as a given logical test remains true. If the logical test returns false on the outset, then no block or actions are repeated.

Do While Statement

This is similar to a while statement except that the statement (or block of code) contained in it will be performed at least once. The logical test is performed after the execution of the program block (i.e. loop) contained in the do-while statement whereas the while statement performs the test first before performing the loop.

For Statement

This is another loop statement. It is also known as the for-loop. With this statement, the number of repetitions will be indicated in the code so you will already know how many times the loop block will be repeated.

For In Statement

This type of loop is just like the for-statement with one slight difference. Instead of the number of loops being indicated numerically, the number of repetitions will be determined by the properties of the object being tested.

For example, you want to repeat certain actions according to the number of colors there are in the rainbow. You can use a for-in statement to perform the actions for every color that is found in a rainbow programming object.

Continue Statement

A continue statement works in tandem with the different looping statements mentioned earlier. What this statement does is that it tells the browser to skip the remaining commands after it and start the loop all over again.

Break Statement

A break statement is also used with the loop statements mentioned earlier. It's like the continue statement except that instead of making the browser repeat the loop, it makes the browser skip all the repetitions and proceed with executing the statements after the loop—essentially breaking out of the loop cycle.

Function Statement

The function statement is used to create a program function (I know, it's not a very creative way to name things but we just can't do anything about it). A function in the world of programming is a group of statements that are designed to perform a specific action or produce a certain result.

An example of this is a block or group of codes that test whether a user has paid for a product or not. Once you declare a function, it can be used in any part of the program that you have written thereby you don't have to write the same lines of code over and over again.

Return Statement

The return statement is used to return the value that is produced by a function.

Var Statement

This statement is used to create a variable.

There are other statements that you will learn as you gain more experience programming with JavaScript. We will cover the above-mentioned statements in detail in the next chapters of this book.

Multiline Comments in JavaScript

In a previous chapter you were shown what comments were and that they are ignored by the browser and not treated as programming code. We also understand that they are used as annotations for the people who read the code.

Another way to use comments is to place them in parts of your programming code or scripts that you want the browser to ignore. To change a statement into a comment all you have to do is to put two forward slashes // to the left of the beginning of the statement. Voila, you have part of the code disabled.

Here's an example of how that is done:

```
1    <!DOCTYPE HTML>
2    <html>
3
4    <body>
5
6      <p>This Has a Comment On It</p>
7
8      <script>
9        alert( 'You won't see part of this text because...' );
10       // alert( 'It has been turned into a comment' );
11         </script>
12
13     <p>And that is how you disable part of your code</p>
14
15   </body>
16
17   </html>
```

N length : 289 lines : 17   Ln : 13 Col : 51 Pos : 264   Windows (CR LF)   UTF-8   INS

However, what if you have multiple lines of code that you want the browser to ignore? Does that mean you need to put comment marks in front of every single one of them? The answer is no. There is another version of comments in JavaScript called multiline comments and they span multiple lines of code as the name implies.

Take a look at the following example:

```
1    /* This is an example
2    Of a multiline comment
3    */
4    alert('There you go folks!');
5    |
```

length : 82   lines : 5   Ln : 5 Col : 1   Pos : 83   Windows (CR LF)   UTF-8   INS

The multiline comment tags are /* ... */" and anything you place in between them will be ignored by the browser. The only rule that you need to remember about multiline comments is that you can't nest them inside one another.

For example, this one is not allowed:

```
/*
 /* this is a nested comment */
*/
alert( 'The example above is not allowed' );
```

If you put these lines of code and try to make a browser interpret them it will produce an error message like "Syntax Error: Unexpected token" or something like that.

Pop Quiz

Questions:

1. What is a statement?
2. What is a loop?
3. Give examples of looping statements
4. How do you temporarily disable parts of your code?
5. What's the difference between single-line comments and multiline comments?

Chapter 6: Variables and Constants

We have touched on variables in the previous chapter and we will go over them in detail in this one. If you remember, there are variables in JavaScript just like we do in algebra and all those other wonderful math subjects.

However, the big difference here is that the variables in JavaScript don't only contain numbers. They can contain other types of data like letters, symbols, and more.

Const versus Let

One rule you have to remember is that before you can use any variable (or any other type of element in your JavaScript) you need to declare it first. Declaring it means that you are setting a memory allocation in your computer's RAM that will be used for that part of your program.

There are two statements that you will need to remember:

- const
- let

We have gone over statements in the previous chapter and we have described some of the statements or commands that you will likely use when you write your scripts or program code. Let's cover the difference between these two statements and how you can use them to create variables.

Here's an example of how you can use const and let to assign values to variables:

```
const pi = 3.1416;

let message = 'Hello';
```

You use the equal sign (also known as the assignment operator) to assign a value to each of these variables. In the case of const in the example above, it assigns the value 3.1416 to pi and let assigns a string of characters to the variable called message. Actually, in this example, pi is not a variable but it is called a constant.

What's the difference?

When you use const the value of the variable is not allowed to change, which is why it's called a constant, to begin with. On the other hand, when you use the let-statement, the value can be changed.

Here's a quick exercise. Type the following code, save it, and open it in your browser.

```
File Edit Search View Encoding Language Settings Tools Macro Run Plugins Window ?                    X

Multiline Comment Example.txt    new 1    testing ulet.html

  1    <html>
  2
  3    <script>
  4        let message;
  5        message = 'Hello!';
  6
  7        alert(message); // shows the variable content
  8    </script>
  9
 10    </html>

length : 127   lines : 10      Ln : 10  Col : 1  Pos : 121        Windows (CR LF)   UTF-8        INS
```

As you can see, the alert statement displays the content of the variable called message. Remember that you don't enclose a variable in quotation marks if you use them as arguments in an alert statement.

Declaring Multiple Variables

Let's say you want to declare multiple variables. You don't need to write a lot of let statements to do that. You can just declare everything using one line, like this:

```
let user = 'Mary', age = 18, message = 'You're late for
                          class!';
```

Separate each variable declaration using a comma. Now, you can also declare them in separate lines, like so:

```
let user = 'Mary',

    age = 18,

    message = 'You're late for class!';
```

Pop Quiz

Question

What do you think is the output of the following code?

```
 1   <html>
 2
 3   <script>
 4       let message;
 5
 6       message = 'Hello!';
 7       alert(message);
 8       message = 'World!';
 9       alert(message);
10   </script>
11
12   </html>
```

Answer:

Two different texts will be displayed even though only one variable was used. Two different values were assigned to the variable and then they were displayed on the screen.

Case in point: the values of variables can be changed or manipulated—meaning you can add, subtract, and edit or alter the contents of a variable.

Two Lets Produces an Error

Try the following code. Type it in Notepad++, save it as HTML, and then open it using a browser.

```
File  Edit  Search  View  Encoding  Language  Settings  Tools  Macro  Run  Plugins  Window  ?                    X

new 1
   1    <html>
   2
   3    <script>
   4        let message = "This";
   5        let message = "That";
   6        alert(message);
   7    </script>
   8
   9    </html>




length : 106   lines : 9      Ln : 6   Col : 20   Pos : 85              Windows (CR LF)    UTF-8                    INS
```

What is displayed on the screen?

If you answered nothing, then you are correct. Why do you think that nothing was displayed even though we had an alert statement there?

It is because **you can't declare the same variable twice**. If you want to change the value of a variable just *declare it once and then use the assignment operator* or equal sign to change the value of the variable.

Rules for Naming Variables

There are only two rules that you should remember when it comes to giving names to the variables that you create in JavaScript:

1. The first character should not be a number.
2. You can only use the letters of the alphabet, numbers 0 to 9, and the symbols _ and $.

As it was mentioned before, JavaScript is case-sensitive. Another thing is that when you use long variable names that have more than one word in them, the usual convention is to use camel case names, like this one:

```
let userName
```

You can capitalize the first letter of the next word.

Note that non-English letters are also allowed in JavaScript but it is not recommended. Here's an example:

```
let имя;
```

Reminder: choose variable names that describe the value that they store. When we name a variable as "password" it should contain passwords. If we name a variable as "monthlySales" then it should contain numbers and the sales figures for the month.

Reserved Words

There are reserved words in JavaScript and you can't use them as variable or constant names. Using them produces an error in your code. Here's the list of reserved words (also known as keywords) in this programming language:

break	const	throw	in
case	continue	delete	instance of
yield	var	do	
function	typeof	super	extends
with	debugge r	switch	finally
catch		new	if
class	default	return	import
while	try	else	for
void	this	export	

These keywords already perform a function in JavaScript, which is why you can't use them as user-generated variable names.

Chapter 7: Data Types and Operators

Variables can contain different types of data. Some are numeric, some are text, and in JavaScript, there are 8 different types of data that you can work with. We will also go over the different operators that you can use to modify the values contained inside the variables.

Dynamically Typed

As it was mentioned early in this book, JavaScript is dynamically typed. That means we can assign numeric values to our variables at the beginning and then assign numbers at a later portion of the code and there won't be any problems. Programming languages that have this property are called dynamically typed.

Now, let's go over the different data types.

Numbers

Numbers in JavaScript can be whole numbers like 100 or 7. They can also be floating-point numbers like

3.1416 or 12.325. You can use the following operators for numeric data:

- + (addition)
- - (subtraction)
- / (division)
- * (multiplication)

Try the following code and see the output in your browser:

```
1    <html>
2
3    <script>
4
5        let x = 5 + 5;
6        alert(x);
7
8    </script>
9
10   </html>
```

length : 74   lines : 10   Ln : 7   Col : 5   Pos : 53   Windows (CR LF)   UTF-8   INS

There are also special numbers that can also be used in JavaScript such as infinity or ∞, and NaN. Add this line to the previous exercise code earlier and see the output:

alert(1 / 0);

NaN on the other hand is the output when you make a computational error. To try that out, add this line to the previous exercise code:

alert("not a number" / 2);

Notice that this statement will return "NaN". If you try to add more computations after it, it will still return NaN. Note that the numbers in JavaScript cover both positive and negative numbers.

BigInt

Note that there is a technical limitation to the range of numbers that can be used in JavaScript. The number data type ranges from $-(2^{53} - 1)$ to $(2^{53} - 1)$. The positive numbers can't be larger than 9,007,199,254,740,991 (same figures in the negative).

If you need a number that is more than that, then you need to convert your number to a BigInt data type. To do that, just add an "n" at the end of the huge number you intend to use, like this one: 9,007,199,254,740,990,321,456n.

Strings

Strings in JavaScript refer to the characters and they are often placed in between single or double quotes, like "Hello" or 'This is an example of a string.'

Note that if you place numbers inside quotes, then numbers like "12345" will be treated as a string or set of characters instead of numbers.

If you want to embed a variable into a string when you output it to the screen, you need to use backticks ` and ` and enclose the expression inside this type of bracket ${...}.

Try this sample code to see how backticks work:

```
1    <html>
2
3      <script>
4
5        let name = "John";
6
7        // embed a variable
8        alert( `Hello, ${name}!` ); // Hello, John!
9
10       // embed an expression
11       alert( `the result is ${1 + 2}` );
12
13      </script>
14
15   </html>
```

length: 203 lines: 15   Ln: 3 Col: 3 Pos: 13   Windows (CR LF)   UTF-8   INS

Note that you can only embed numbers or mathematical expressions using backticks. If you change the backticks in the previous sample and use single or double quotes, you can't embed either the expression or the mathematical formula and they will be treated as text.

Boolean Data Type

Other than numbers and strings, another useful data type is Boolean. You can use this data type for testing the logic of certain expressions. It helps in decision-making statements.

Boolean data can either be true or false.

Embed the following code in an HTML file and open it in a browser:

```
let isGreater = 5 > 1;

alert( isGreater );
```

Notice that the output of this script is "true". The variable isGreater is assigned a value of true because 5 is greater than 1. We use comparison operators like > (greater than), < (less than), != (not equal to) and equal to (==) to make these logical tests. Another logical operator is "||" which means "or". The or-operator will always return true if either of the two items being compared is true. It will only return false if both items being compared are false.

Another operator that you should become familiar with is the && (And) operator. Remember that in the world of computers which speak in ones and zeroes, the number 1 is true and zero is false. Well, technically, any positive number is true and zero is false.

So, that means a variable that has a value of 1, when tested logically will return true. If it has a value of zero, then it returns false.

Going back to the && operator, here is a sample expression:

```
alert( 1 && 0 ); // 0
```

The && operator evaluates the operand at the left and then the one at the right. In this example, the && operator will return a zero or false. Why? This is because it will look for the first false value, which is why the alert statement above will display false or zero.

Check out this next example:

```
alert( 1 && 5 ); // 5
```

Notice that the && operator returns a 5 or true. What it does is that it evaluates all the operands from left to right (i.e. 1 and then 5). In this case, there is no zero so there no false value. If that is the case then it will return the last true value (i.e. 5).

Null

The null value assigns an empty value to a variable or value unknown. This is a great way to initialize variables to make sure they don't contain garbage data from memory. You can assign a null value to a variable like this:

```
let score = null;
```

Undefined

If you forget to assign a value to a variable and try to use it in math expressions, logical comparisons, or just display it to the screen, your browser will automatically return "undefined", which means that there is no value assigned to that variable.

Try the following code and see what output you get:

```
1   <html>
2
3     <script>
4
5       let age;
6
7       alert(age);
8
9     </script>
10
11  </html>
```

length : 76   lines : 11   Ln : 7   Col : 5   Pos : 39   Windows (CR LF)   UTF-8   INS

Object Data Type

We will only introduce the object data type here. All of the data types that you have seen so far only contain one value. These data types are called primitive data types.

A more advanced data type that is used in JavaScript and other programming languages is an object, and this type of data can contain more than one value.

Think of it this way, you can create a variable that can represent different customer records. The record can contain several bits of information (or values) such as the customer's name, phone number, address, email, social media accounts, and transactions.

You can store all of that information in an object and you can create one for every customer. That way you can organize data and easily locate the information for each customer as it becomes needful.

Symbols

The last data type we will go over is called a symbol. This one is used to create identifiers for objects.

Pop Quiz

Task

Try to guess the output of each line on this script:

```
1    let name = "Ilya";
2
3    alert( `hello ${1}` ); // ?
4
5    alert( `hello ${"name"}` ); // ?
6
7    alert( `hello ${name}` ); // ?
```

length : 119   lines : 7   Ln : 7   Col : 31   Pos : 120   Windows (CR LF)   UTF-8   INS

After guessing, embed that script in an HTML file and
see the result if you have answered correctly.

Chapter 8: Interacting with Your Users

Early on in this book, we mentioned that JavaScript makes websites and web applications more interactive. We have already shown you examples where we have scripts that create buttons on the screen.

You have also tried the alert statement which displays stuff on the screen. We will go over a couple more interactive features in detail. Remember that we will only deal with the basics and not the complex interactive features of JavaScript.

Creating a Prompt

From what we have learned so far, using the alert statement only displays a small pop-up on the screen. This small popup is also known as a modal window. When we say modal, it means that it is something that the user can interact with.

In the case of the alert statement, all that a user can do is click the "ok" button. To make things more interactive, you can ask the user to enter certain information. We now introduce you to the prompt function. Don't worry too much about what a function is for now. We will go over functions in a later chapter.

The syntax of the prompt function goes like this:

prompt(title, [default]);

The keyword prompt is followed by an opening and closing parenthesis "(" and ")". Inside it are two arguments. An argument is a programming term that means that it is a value that can affect the behavior of a function.

In this case, the "title" is the text that you use to tell the user what to enter. The [default] part is the default value that will be displayed. Note that this second argument is optional.

To see how a prompt works, try the following code and open it in your browser:

```
1   <html>
2
3     <script>
4
5       let userName = prompt('What is your name?');
6
7       alert(`Hello ${userName}!`);
8
9     </script>
10
11  </html>
```

length : 135   lines : 11   Ln : 7   Col : 30   Pos : 106   Windows (CR LF)   UTF-8   INS

Quick Question: what if the user does not enter anything or just clicks cancel? If that is the case then the prompt function will return null.

Confirm Function

The confirm function also shows a modal window just like the alert and prompt functions. It has the following syntax:

confirm(question);

The keyword here is confirmed and it has one argument called the question. This argument is a prompt that will make the user choose to click either "OK" or "Cancel" in the modal window. Clicking "OK" will return a true value while clicking "Cancel" will return false.

Try the following exercise:

```
1    <html>
2
3      <script>
4
5        let currentFeeling = confirm("Do you feel OK?");
6
7        alert( currentFeeling );
8
9      </script>
10
11   </html>
```

length : 128   lines : 11   Ln : 11   Col : 8   Pos : 129   Windows (CR LF)   UTF-8   INS

So far, what we have learned only shows us a linear execution of our commands and instructions. In the next chapter, we will see how JavaScript can be made to decide on certain things and then take different courses of action depending on the logical tests that will be made.

Chapter 9: Conditional Statements

Sometimes your program code needs to perform different actions depending on certain conditions. For example, your system may have to decide which content a user should be given access to depending on certain restrictions.

If it's a premium user then they should be given access to most of the site's content. If it's just a site visitor then they can only be given access to a few of the pages and given a link to the signup page. If it is a site administrator then they should be given access to all the content including the backend settings of the website itself.

This is where conditional statements come in.

The If Statement

To facilitate this decision making and action branching, you need to use the if-statement or if function. Consider the following example:

```
<html>

    <script>
        let snowColor = prompt('What is the color of snow?', '');

        if (snowColor == 'white') alert( 'You are right!' );


    </script>

</html>
```

Did you notice the ' ' at the end of the prompt statement on line 4? That is used to initialize the default value in its syntax to display an empty prompt box.

From this example, we see that if the user entered the right answer, the message "you are right" will be displayed. However, what if the user entered the wrong answer? There should be a set of instructions or statements that should cover that, right? The answer to that is the else clause.

Else Clause

The else clause is a part of the if-statement. It is optional but it gives you an option to provide a separate set of commands that can be performed if the condition set in the if statement is not met (i.e. it returns false).

Here's an example of how this works; try the following code:

From this example, we can see that all statements inside the { } after the if-statement will be performed if the condition year == 1912 returns true. But if it does not, the statements inside the { } after the else clause will be executed.

Else If Clause

JavaScript allows you to add more conditional statements before the else clause. This allows you to create more options in case there are certain conditions that you need to cover as well.

Here's an example of how to use an else-if clause:

```
<html>

<script>
    let year = prompt('What year did the Titanic sink?', '');

    if (year < 1912) {
        alert( 'Too early!' );
    } else if (year > 1912) {
        alert( 'Too late' );
    } else {
        alert( 'You guessed it right!' );
    }
</script>

</html>
```

The if-statement first tests the value of the variable year. It will have three possible outcomes: one for earlier than 1912, later than 1912, and exactly 1912.

The ? Conditional Operator

You are allowed to use more else-if statements as long as you have more conditions to test and have courses of action for each of those conditions. Here's an example of how multiple else-ifs would be used:

```
*new 2 - Notepad++                                          —  □  X
File  Edit  Search  View  Encoding  Language  Settings  Tools  Macro  Run  Plugins  Window  ?   X

new 2

  1    <html>
  2
  3    <script>
  4
  5      if (age < 3) {
  6      message = 'Hi, baby!';
  7      } else if (age < 18) {
  8      message = 'Hello!';
  9      } else if (age < 100) {
 10      message = 'Greetings!';
 11      } else {
 12      message = 'What an unusual age!';
 13      }
 14
 15    </script>
 16
 17    </html>

length : 243   lin Ln : 13   Col : 2   Pos : 216        Windows (CR LF)    UTF-8              INS
```

As you can see, this is already a bit of a long bit of code and it can be confusing at times. JavaScript has the conditional operator "?" that you can use to simplify such long if-else statements.

Try the following sample code:

```
*new 2 - Notepad++                                          —  □  X
File  Edit  Search  View  Encoding  Language  Settings  Tools  Macro  Run  Plugins  Window  ?   X

new 2

  1    <html>
  2
  3    <script>
  4
  5      let age = prompt('age?', 18);
  6
  7      let message = (age < 3) ? 'Hi, baby!' :
  8      (age < 18) ? 'Hello!' :
  9      (age < 100) ? 'Greetings!' :
 10      'What an unusual age!';
 11
 12      alert( message );
 13    </script>
 14
 15    </html>
 16

length : 241   lin Ln : 14   Col : 1   Pos : 231        Windows (CR LF)    UTF-8              INS
```

Take note that this example with the question mark conditional operator gives you the same result as the previous else-if code that you tried earlier. The difference is that this one is simpler than the previous one.

Pop Quiz

Task 1

Use the if-statement and its related clauses and conditional operators. Write a script that asks the user to enter a number and prompt that use that the script will tell whether it is positive or negative.

Test the number that was entered using a comparison operator. Output to the screen whether the number that was entered is positive, a negative number, or zero.

Note that we only assume that the user will always enter a number There are ways to check if they entered a number or not but we won't go over that for now.

Task 2

Rewrite the following code using the "?" conditional operator instead of using if-statements.

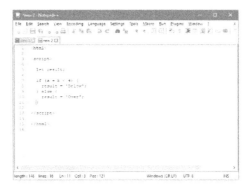

Answer to Pop Quiz Task 1

```
3   <script>
4
5       let value = prompt('Type a number
6       and I'll tell you if it is positive or negative', 0);
7
8   if (value > 0) {
9       alert( 'It is positive' );
10  } else if (value < 0) {
11      alert( 'It is negative' );
12  } else {
13      alert( 'It is zero' );
14  }
15
16  </script>
17
18  </html>
19
```

Answer to Pop Quiz Task 2

```
1   <html>
2
3   <script>
4
5     let result = (a + b < 4) ? 'Below' : 'Over';
6
7   </script>
8
9   </html>
10
```

Chapter 10: Looping Statements

One of the functions that we mentioned and described earlier in chapter 5 when we discussed the different statements in JavaScript is looping statements. Two of the statements that we described in that chapter are the while- and for-loops. We will go over these two loops in this chapter.

What is a Loop?

Earlier, we described a loop as something that repeats. In programming, a block that is composed of several lines of statements can be repeated over and over if they are placed within a loop. This way you don't have to repeat them over and over if all you need is to repeat the same action.

The While Loop

As it was described earlier, a while loop tests a condition first and then performs a block of code or statements as long as the condition remains true. It is inferred that the result of the conditional test can change during the execution of the statements inside the loop.

Here is the syntax for this loop:

```
while (condition) {
  // code
  // so-called "loop body"
}
```

Here's an example of a while loop:

Try that code and open it in your browser. The while-loop on line 6 will test the value of the variable i. If its value is less than 3 then the statements inside the { } will be executed (the loop body). Inside the loop, the body has two statements.

The first one displays the value of the variable i and the second statement increases the value of the variable i by 1. That is what is meant by "i++". Take note that the ++ operator will increment the value of an integer by 1. When the value of i is no longer less than 3, then the loop breaks and moves on to the next line in the program code. In this case, the program terminates when it hits line 11 to 13.

Note that if the ++ operator increments by one, the -- operator on the other hand decrements number values by 1.

Try this next code that uses the -- operator to decrement the value of the number:

Notice that in this example we use the statement while (i). This is a short way of writing while(i != 0). This is because in the world of computers and programming the number 1 denotes true and zero denotes false.

Single Statement Loops

Note that if your loop only has one statement inside it, you don't need to enclose it in curly braces { }. See the following example:

```
let i = 3
```

```
while (i) alert(i--);
```

Endless Loop

Be careful when writing the conditions for the while loop. You should also make sure that there is a way to break the loop or else you will be stuck in an endless cycle. Well, technically not endless—that is only until the computer runs out of RAM to be exact.

In our previous example of the while loop in action (i.e. the one that uses i++), if you remove the i++ on line 8, the value of the variable i won't change at all, and the loop will cycle on continuously (in theory, that is).

Do...While Loop

As it was explained earlier, this loop is the opposite of the while loop. The loop body is executed first and then the logical test is performed after. It has the following syntax:

```
do {
 // loop body
} while (condition);
```

Try this sample code in Notepad++ to see how it works:

```
<html>

<script>

   let i = 0;
   do {
     alert( i );
     i++;
   } while (i < 3);

</script>

</html>
```

Notice, from the example above, given the logic of the do...while loop, the statements in the loop body will be performed at least once. If the value of i was initially 3 then the loop terminates after displaying its value once on the screen.

The For-Loop

With the for-loop, the number of repetitions will be indicated at the beginning of the loop so you will already know how many times the statement in the loop body will be repeated.

This loop statement has the following syntax:

```
for (begin; conditional test; step) {
   // ... body of the loop...
   }
```

Note that this loop is more complex than the other two that we have tried. However, since this type of loop provides a lot more control, it is one of the most used looping methods in JavaScript and other programming languages as well.

Here's an example of the for-loop in action:

Let's go over this loop step by step so you will understand what's going on. The loop begins on line 5. What it does is that it assigns the value of zero to the variable x—i.e. the let statement in line 5.

It then makes a logical test for the value of x < 3. What this means is that the for-loop is going to count from zero to 2.

If the condition returns true (which is correct at the beginning the loop), then the loop body is executed.

If it returns false, then the for-loop terminates. At the end of line 5 the value of x is incremented by 1 via x++.

Inline Variables

Note that in the case of these loops, the counting variable that we used such as i and x, were created within the loop code. As such they only exist inside the loop. In other words, they can only be used within the loop body.

If you use them outside of the loop, then it will produce an error. These local variables that exist within the body of a statement are called an inline variable. They are local variables and they only work inside the statement that created them.

To test that, run the following code in your browser. Notice that it will produce an error.

```
<html>

<script>

  for (let i = 0; i < 3; i++) {
    alert(i); // displays the numbers 0, 1, 2
  }
  alert(i); // this line produces an  error

</script>

</html>
```

As you can see from the example above, line 8 will generate an error. It uses the inline variable i that only exists inside the for-loop.

Global and Local Variables

One way to avoid this is to just declare the variable outside of the loop and then use that global variable, which can be used inside a loop anyway. Remember that there are global variables and local variables. You can use global variables pretty much anywhere in your code but local variables can only be used within the function or statement where they were made.

Here's a quick solution to the problematic code in the previous example.

In this solution, the variable i is declared in line 4 before the loop was started in line 6, making it a global variable that can be used anywhere in your code. Its value changes as the loop iterates since the for-loop uses it as a kind of counter for the loop iterations. When the loop closes, the new value of i will be displayed via the alert statement in line 10 with no problems.

Break and Continue Statements

In chapter 5 we described the break continue statements as code that you can put within the loop to skip loop iterations. The break statement stops the loop completely while a continue statement will only skip one loop iteration.

To demonstrate the difference between these two, try the following example. The first one is for the break statement:

```
<html>
<script>

    let sum = 0;

    while (true) {
      let value = +prompt("Enter a number", '');

        if (!value) break; // (*)

      sum += value;
    }

    alert( 'Sum: ' + sum );

</script>
</html>
```

The break statement in line 9 will stop the loop completely.

This next example is for the continue statement:

```
<html>
<script>

    for (let i = 0; i < 10; i++) {

      // if true, skip the remaining part of the body
      if (i % 2 == 0) continue;

      alert(i); // 1, then 3, 5, 7, 9
    }

</script>
</html>
```

Notice that when the condition in line 7 is fulfilled that iteration is skipped, which means the alert statement in line 9 is not performed for that time only.

Pop Quiz

Task 1

You can rewrite code using one loop for another. The sample code below uses a for-loop. I want you to edit the code and this time use a while-loop instead of a for-loop. You should come up with the same results even though you used a different loop.

```
1   <html>
2   <script>
3
4       for (let i = 0; i < 3; i++) {
5           alert( `number ${i}!` );
6       }
7
8   </script>
9   </html>
10
```

Task 2

Write a script that continuously prompts the user to enter a number that is higher than 100. The loop will only terminate if the user enters a number that is higher than 100.

Answer to Pop Quiz Task 1

```
<html>
<script>

  let i = 0;
    while (i < 3) {
    alert( `number ${i}!` );
    i++;
  }

</script>
</html>
```

Answer to Pop Quiz Task 2

```
<html>
<script>

  let num;

  do {
    num = prompt("Enter a number greater than 100?", 0);
  } while (num <= 100 && num);

</script>
</html>
```

Note: look at the condition on line 8. The && operator is used as a contingency against the possibility that the user will click the Cancel button.

When that button is clicked, the variable num will have a null value and is not necessarily less than 100. Since the expression 100 && null returns false, it will terminate the loop instead of proceeding with another iteration.

Chapter 11: Functions

You have been using functions in your scripts so far like alert, prompt, and confirm. JavaScript allows you to create your functions. Remember, as it was defined earlier, a function is a collection of statements and these statements are designed to perform a specific task.

These functions that you will write are called user-defined functions.

Here's an example of one that adds numbers:

```
<html>
<script>

   function sum(a, b) {
      return a + b;
   }

   let result = sum(1, 2);
      alert( result ); // 3

</script>
</html>
```

From this example, you can see that the function declaration is on line 4 using the keyword "function". Again, that isn't a creative way to name things—we create functions using function—but that's what we've got so we just have to use it.

Okay, moving on, the syntax of a function declaration goes like this:

```
function name(parameters) {
  ...body...
}
```

Going back to our example earlier, the name of the function is sum. It is followed by certain parameters or arguments, which can change the output of a function as was explained in an earlier chapter.

The body of the function, just like a loop body, is found in between the curly brackets { }. This setup looks familiar because you've been doing it for a bit now when you worked on the looping statements earlier.

The big difference here is that a function does more than just repeat steps or statements. They perform a certain function (told you it's a bad naming convention). In the case of our example above, the sum function that we created adds up the values of a and b.

Notice on line 5 we have what is called a return statement. It can be placed anywhere in the function body. What it does is that it takes the value of that expression and it produces the output of the function that you created.

In the case of the example above, it returns the sum of the two numbers that were entered as arguments to the function called sum. You can use variables in those two arguments and you can ask users to enter the values for those arguments. You can also just compute the values of those arguments. There are lots of possibilities that you can go for in the design of your very own functions.

Reminder: Local and Global Variables

Again, just like what we have already mentioned in the previous chapter, you can declare variables inside functions, which will be considered as local variables. Remember that these variables only function or exist within the body of the function that you create.

If you use them outside of the function body then that will cause a bug or error. You can mitigate against this by using global variables.

Pop Quiz

Task

Let's assume that we are designing a video streaming site, just like Netflix. However, we want to check whether the user who is signing up for a subscription is old enough since there are age restrictions for these sites.

Create a script that will prompt users to enter their age. In that script, write a function that will evaluate whether a user is 18 years old or below. If the user is age 18 and above then output a message that says "Access granted" if not then send out a message that says "Access denied".

Answer to Pop Quiz

```
<html>
<script>

  function checkAge(age) {
    if (age >= 18) {
      return true;
    } else {
      return confirm('Do you have permission from your parents?');
      }
    }

let age = prompt('How old are you?', 18);

if ( checkAge(age) ) {
  alert( 'Access granted' );
} else {
  alert( 'Access denied' );
}

</script>
</html>
```

Conclusion

Thank you once again for downloading this book. After learning all the subjects that have been discussed and working on the different exercises and quizzes provided here, you should have some preliminary knowledge about JavaScript programming.

Remember that we have only touched on the core basics of this scripting language. There is a lot more that it can do. This book was designed for absolute beginners and at this point, you are no longer one.

You have dipped your proverbial toes in the wonderful world of web coding and computer programming in general.

If you find that writing code is absolutely fun, then you can venture further into JavaScript learning more intermediate and advanced subjects such as objects, code style, debugging, automated testing, object references, JSON methods, arrays, prototypal inheritances, error handling, UI events, and document and resource loading among many other things.

The possibilities are endless and JavaScript is just one of many other languages thus far. I would also recommend that you should master HTML and CSS since you've dabbled in them slightly as you went along with the exercises in this book. Another programming language that is also pretty easy to learn is Python, which has a plethora of applications as well. If you like you can also move forward to more advanced and stricter languages that we mentioned in this book.

Once again, thank you for going over the lessons in this fundamental programming guide. May you find your journey into coding to be something truly wonderful. Who knows; you may even find coding as a satisfying career change.

www.ingramcontent.com/pod-product-compliance
Lightning Source LLC
LaVergne TN
LVHW051706050326
832903LV00032B/4038